MAKE A STAR LIGHT!

And More Circuitry Challenges

Rebecca Felix

**Consulting Editor, Diane Craig,
M.A./Reading Specialist**

Super Sandcastle

An Imprint of Abdo Publishing
abdobooks.com

abdobooks.com

Published by Abdo Publishing, a division of ABDO, PO Box 398166, Minneapolis, Minnesota 55439. Copyright © 2021 by Abdo Consulting Group, Inc. International copyrights reserved in all countries. No part of this book may be reproduced in any form without written permission from the publisher. Super SandCastle™ is a trademark and logo of Abdo Publishing.

Printed in the United States of America, North Mankato, Minnesota
102020
012021

THIS BOOK CONTAINS
RECYCLED MATERIALS

Design: Kelly Doudna, Mighty Media, Inc.
Production: Mighty Media, Inc.
Editor: Liz Salzmann
Cover Photographs: Mighty Media, Inc.; Shutterstock Images (boy)
Interior Photographs: Mighty Media, Inc., pp. 10, 11, 15, 16, 17, 18, 19, 20, 21, 22, 26, 27, 28, 29; Mike Mozart/Flickr, p. 12; Peter DaSilva/Flickr, p. 6; Rob Pegoraro/Flickr, p. 13; Shutterstock Images, pp. 4, 7, 8, 9, 11 (electrical wires), 13 (drone), 23, 24, 25, 28 (boy), 30
Design Elements: Mighty Media, Inc.; Shutterstock Images

The following manufacturers/names appearing in this book are trademarks:
Artist's Loft™, Duracell®, Glue Dots®, Philips®

Library of Congress Control Number: 2020940303

Publisher's Cataloging-in-Publication Data

Names: Felix, Rebecca, author.
Title: Make a star light! and more circuitry challenges / by Rebecca Felix
Description: Minneapolis, Minnesota : Abdo Publishing, 2021 | Series: Super simple makerspace STEAM challenge
Identifiers: ISBN 9781532194399 (lib. bdg.) | ISBN 9781098213756 (ebook)
Subjects: LCSH: Handicraft for children--Juvenile literature. | Electric circuits--Juvenile literature. | Light—Juvenile literature. | Electricity—Juvenile literature. | Technology--Juvenile literature.
Classification: DDC 745.5--dc23

Super SandCastle™ books are created by a team of professional educators, reading specialists, and content developers around five essential components—phonemic awareness, phonics, vocabulary, text comprehension, and fluency—to assist young readers as they develop reading skills and strategies and increase their general knowledge. All books are written, reviewed, and leveled for guided reading and early reading intervention programs for use in shared, guided, and independent reading and writing activities to support a balanced approach to literacy instruction.

TO ADULT HELPERS

The challenges in this book can be done using common crafting materials and household items. To keep kids safe, provide assistance with sharp or hot objects. Be sure to protect clothing and work surface from messy supplies. Be ready to offer guidance during brainstorming and assist when necessary.

CONTENTS

BECOME A MAKER

A makerspace is like a laboratory. It's a place where ideas are formed and problems are solved. Kids like you create amazing things in makerspaces. Many makerspaces are in schools and libraries. But they can also be in kitchens, bedrooms, and backyards. Anywhere can be a makerspace when you use imagination, inspiration, **collaboration**, and problem-solving!

IMAGINATION

This takes you to new places and lets you experience new things. Anything is possible with imagination!

INSPIRATION

This is the spark that gives you an idea. Inspiration can come from almost anywhere!

Makerspace Toolbox

COLLABORATION

Makers work together. They ask questions and get ideas from everyone around them. **Collaboration** solves problems that seem impossible.

PROBLEM-SOLVING

Things often don't go as planned when you're creating. But that's part of the fun! Find creative **solutions** to any problem that comes up. These will make your project even better.

CHALLENGE: CIRCUITRY

How often do you flip a light switch, turn on a computer, or charge a device such as a smartphone? These actions are all possible because of circuitry!

A circuit is a closed path of an electric current. Circuits can be small and simple or large and **complicated**. Circuit systems make lights and outlets work throughout buildings. Electrical engineers **design**, build, and maintain circuits of all sizes.

MEET AN ELECTRICAL ENGINEER

Yoky Matsuoka is an electrical engineer and computer scientist. In 2009, Matsuoka was one of three people working at technology company Google who founded Google X. This branch of Google **develops** new electronics ideas. Today, Matsuoka is a leader at electronics company Panasonic. There, she works on smart **appliances** that connect to home circuitry.

Electrical engineers wire light systems in **stadiums**.

Electrical engineers set up, test, and maintain circuits in space **satellites**.

Electrical engineers **design** circuits to power robotic arms that help build cars.

CHALLENGE EXTENDED

Electrical engineers are challenged by demands. Demands are needs or desires that must be met. Electrical engineers are also challenged by limits. These might be time limits or space limits. Electrical engineers might also be limited by what materials they can use. The key is figuring out how to meet demands while working within any limits.

Are you ready to be an electrical engineer in your makerspace? Read on to find out how the challenges in this book work!

HOW IT WORKS

THERE ARE FOUR CHALLENGES IN THIS BOOK. EACH CHALLENGE PRESENTS A TASK TO COMPLETE.

THE TASK WILL COME WITH AT LEAST ONE DEMAND OR LIMIT. THAT'S WHAT MAKES IT A CHALLENGE!

EACH CHALLENGE WILL HAVE MORE DIFFICULT DEMANDS AND LIMITS THAN THE LAST. THAT'S WHY IT'S A GOOD IDEA TO START WITH CHALLENGE 1 AND WORK UP TO CHALLENGE 4.

MORE MINDS

Invite others to tackle these challenges with you! You can work together as a group. Or, you can work individually and compare results.

ALUMINUM FOIL

GATHER YOUR MATERIALS

There are a few materials you'll need to do the electrical engineering challenges in this book.

BATTERY

LEDs

IMAGINE

IT'S UP TO YOU WHAT ADDITIONAL MATERIALS YOU USE. EVERY MAKERSPACE HAS DIFFERENT SUPPLIES. WHAT'S IN YOUR SPACE? GATHER MATERIALS THAT YOU CAN USE FOR STRUCTURE, CONNECTING, AND DECORATION.

STRUCTURE

These materials provide your creation with shape and support.

3VDC MOTOR

ELECTRICAL WIRES

ELECTRICAL TAPE

SCISSORS

CONNECTING
These materials help connect the different parts of your creation.

DECORATIONS & DETAILS
These materials add fun **details** that make your creation stand out.

Glue DOTS
mini

11

REAL ELECTRICAL ENGINEERS, REAL CHALLENGES

Before you take on your circuitry challenges, get inspired! Start by discovering some real-world challenges that electrical engineers have faced. Check out the amazing results of these challenges!

CHALLENGE: CREATE HOME LIGHTING THAT CAN BE CONTROLLED WIRELESSLY.

RESULT: PHILLIPS HUE BULBS, INVENTED IN 2012. IN 2019, NEW **VERSIONS** OF THE BULBS INCLUDED BLUETOOTH. USERS CONTROL THEM WITH SMARTPHONE APPS AND VOICE COMMANDS.

CHALLENGE:
DESIGN A TELEVISION ABLE TO DISPLAY VIDEOS **HORIZONTALLY** OR **VERTICALLY**.

RESULT:
SAMSUNG SERO, A FLAT-SCREEN TELEVISION THAT ROTATES BASED ON THE SHAPE OF THE VIDEO BEING DISPLAYED.

CHALLENGE:
BUILD A MACHINE THAT CAN MAKE DELIVERIES, TAKE PHOTOS, AND PROVIDE MAPS AND DIRECTIONS.

RESULT:
DRONES THAT ALLOW USERS TO MAP LAND, DELIVER PACKAGES, AND EXPLORE AREAS WITHOUT ACTUALLY BEING PRESENT. SOME CHINESE DRONES EVEN CARRY PEOPLE AS FLYING TAXIS!

IMAGINE

CAN YOU THINK OF OTHER POSSIBLE SOLUTIONS TO THESE CHALLENGES? WHAT IS THE WILDEST IDEA YOU CAN COME UP WITH?

13

CHALLENGE ACCEPTED!

HERE'S SOME ADVICE FOR TACKLING THE CHALLENGES IN THIS BOOK:

1. **LOOK BEYOND THE MAKERSPACE.** The perfect material might be in your garage, kitchen, or toy chest.

2. **ASK FOR HELP.** Share ideas with friends and family. Ask them for their ideas. Starting with many minds can lead you to places you'd never go on your own!

3. **THINK IT THROUGH.** Don't give up when things don't go exactly as planned. Instead, think about the problem you are having. What are some ways to solve it?

4. **BE CONFIDENT.** You may not know right away how you'll meet a challenge. But trust that you will come up with a **solution**. Start every challenge by saying, "Challenge Accepted!"

Do you have the materials you need? Are you inspired by the work of electrical engineers? Then read on for your first challenge!

SHINY CIRCUIT CREATURE

TASK: Construct a working circuit inside a creature.

aluminum foil

HINT
Start by making your circuit. Connect wires to aluminum foil, and connect the foil to a button battery.

✓ DEMAND
The creature must include at least one bulb or LED that lights up.

✗ LIMIT
The circuit must use aluminum foil as a conductor.

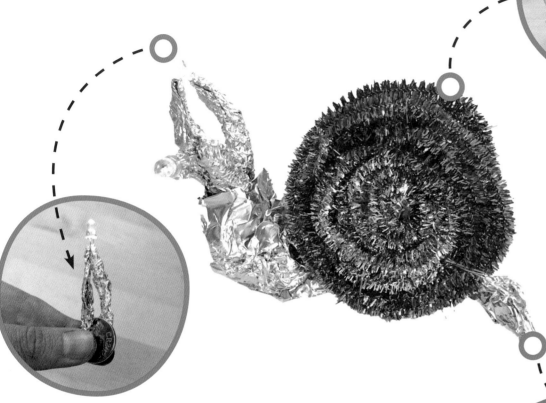

Chenille stems form a sparkly snail shell. Glue dots attach it to the body.

Aluminum foil not only connects the circuit. It forms the creature's body too.

Strips of aluminum foil make the LED wires longer.

HINT
Test the circuit. Hold the battery between the foil strips. If the LED doesn't light up, turn the battery around between the strips.

BUZZER BUTTON

TASK: Create a button that buzzes when pressed.

PRESS

battery

buzzer

4"

4"

springs?

✓	✗
DEMAND All circuitry must be hidden inside the button.	**LIMIT** The completed button's dimensions must not be bigger than 4 inches (10 cm) in any direction.

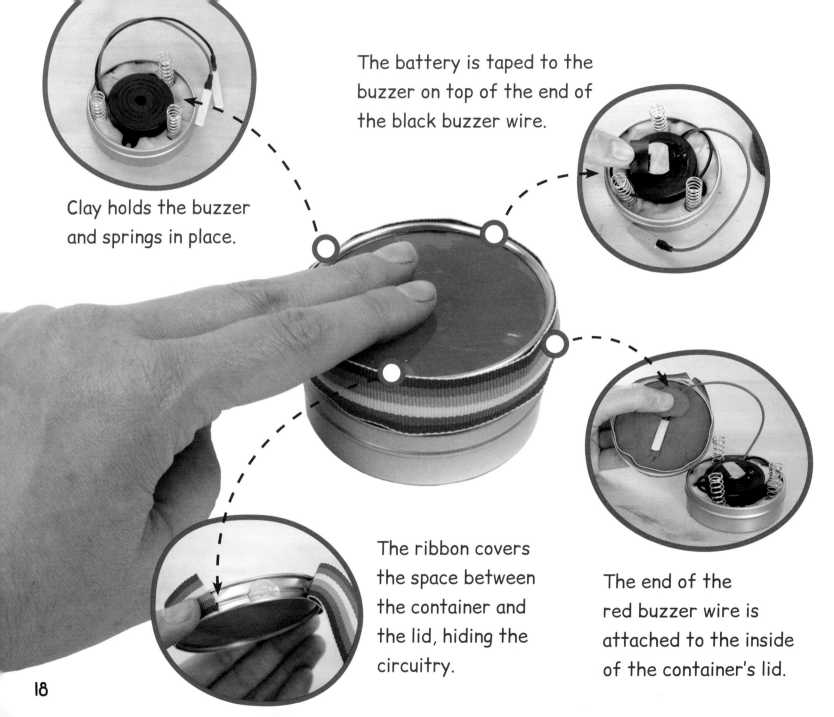

Clay holds the buzzer and springs in place.

The battery is taped to the buzzer on top of the end of the black buzzer wire.

The ribbon covers the space between the container and the lid, hiding the circuitry.

The end of the red buzzer wire is attached to the inside of the container's lid.

MOBILE BOT

TASK: Build a robot.

Styrofoam

Legs —
3? 4?

HINT

Use a **vibrating** motor, such as a buzzer. Before building your bot, hold the motor wires against the battery to test that the circuit works.

✓ DEMAND

The bot must move.

✓ DEMAND

The bot must have legs and eyes.

✗ LIMIT

You must complete the task in 80 minutes or less.

Styrofoam, toothpicks, and foil tissue paper are lightweight enough to be moved by the **vibrations** of the buzzers.

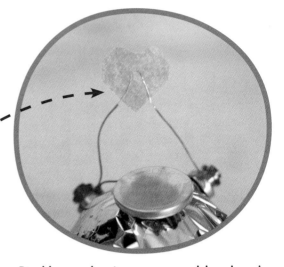

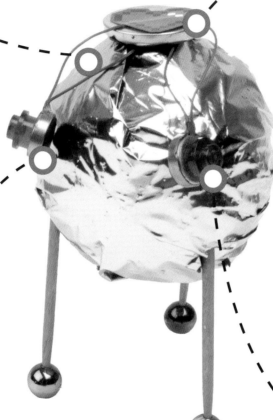

Both red wires are attached to a sticker. The blue wires are under the battery. Pressing the sticker to the battery completes the circuit. The robot moves! Removing the sticker stops the robot.

Two small buzzers provide power without adding much weight.

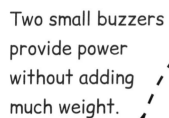

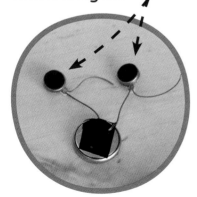

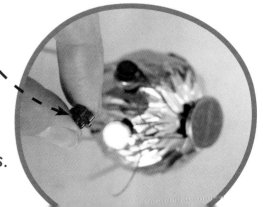

Plastic circles glued to the buzzers form the robot's eyes.

CHALLENGE 4:
STAR LIGHT

TASK: Make a glowing star light.

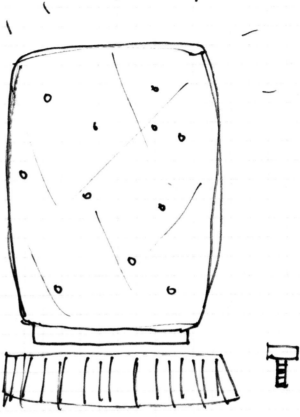

✓ **DEMAND**
The light must have an on-off switch.

✓ **DEMAND**
There must be a way to replace the battery.

✗ **LIMIT**
The light's structure must be made entirely from recycled materials.

Painting newspaper blue and black makes it look like the night sky. Swirls of glitter give it a starry look!

Holes punched in strips of newspaper let light through and look like stars.

One wire goes from the battery to the bolt. Another wire goes from the battery to the washer. Placing the washer over the bolt completes the circuit. The light turns on!

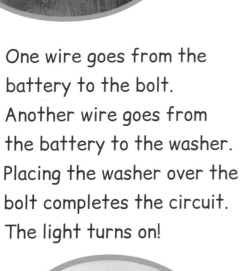

The newspaper strips are glued to the jar. A layer of glue is brushed over them. It dries clear.

HOW DID YOU DO?

After you've completed each challenge, think about how it went.

WHAT IS ANOTHER WAY YOU COULD HAVE APPROACHED THE SAME CHALLENGE?

WHAT WAS THE MOST DIFFICULT PART OF THE CHALLENGE?

WHAT WOULD HAVE MADE THE TASK EASIER?

WHAT KINDS OF PROBLEMS CAME UP, AND HOW DID YOU SOLVE THEM?

GET INSPIRED

As a makerspace electrical engineer, you can find inspiration nearly anywhere. This will help you approach your challenges with a ton of ideas!

LOOK AT NATURE

Electricity occurs naturally in many ways. Static electricity is created by **friction**. Electricity comes from lightning too. One lightning bolt can hold one **billion volts** of electricity! Some animals give off electricity as a form of protection. Electric eels can produce an electric shock strong enough to stop a predator much larger than itself!

LOOK AT DEVICES & APPLIANCES

You likely use devices and **appliances** powered by electric circuits every day! Smartphones, tablets, and watches all use electricity. Look around your home or school. What electronic devices and appliances do you see? Televisions, computers, and microwaves also use electric circuits.

LOOK AT CITIES

Cities use large, **complicated** networks of electric circuitry for power. Look for power lines and poles along roads. The wires form large circuits that bring electricity to homes and businesses. Wiring in these buildings creates circuits for lights and power outlets. Traffic lights and streetlights also use electric circuits.

Do these examples inspire you to create more complicated circuits of your own?

HELPFUL HACKS

As you work, you might discover ways to make challenging tasks easier. Keep these simple tricks and **techniques** in mind as you work through your circuitry challenges.

Use electrical tape to connect the parts of your circuits. It is made to withstand heat from lights, wires, and batteries.

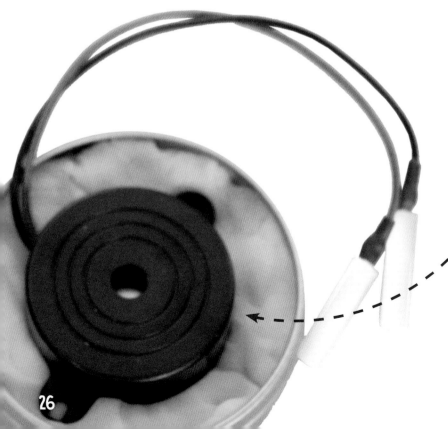

Try using materials that can be shaped to hold the buzzer circuitry in place. Then, you can easily change it if the connections don't line up right.

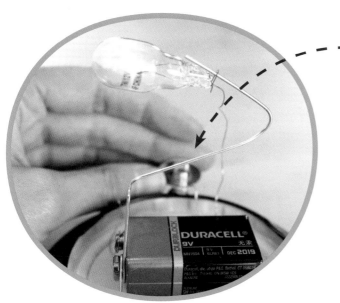

Always test your circuit before building a structure around it. Then you won't have to take the structure apart if the circuit needs to be fixed.

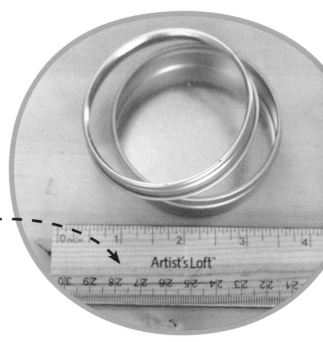

If a challenge includes a size limit, measure your structure before you make any connections that can't be undone.

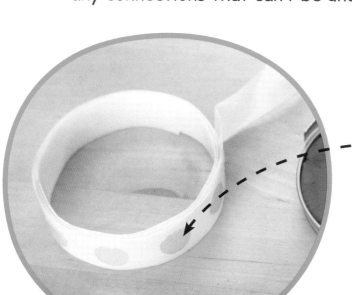

Glue dots are less messy than liquid glue when working with small electrical parts such as wires and batteries.

PROBLEM-SOLVING

You'll probably run into problems as you attempt the challenges in this book. Instead of giving up, open your mind to new ideas. You'll likely find more than one **solution** to your problem!

PROBLEM

Your light bulb, battery, and wires are all brand-new. But the bulb won't light up when they're all connected!

THINK

Why did this happen? Maybe the **voltage** of the battery is too weak or powerful for the voltage of the bulb.

BRAINSTORM AND TEST

Try coming up with three possible **solutions** to any problem. Maybe your bot didn't move. You could:

1. Try using lighter materials.

2. Check that the bot's body materials aren't dragging or getting caught on the surface the bot is trying to move across.

3. Try adding another motor and battery to the circuit to give the bot more power.

SOLUTION

Compare the **voltage** on the battery and bulb packaging. The two numbers should be about the same.

A NEW DAY, A NEW CHALLENGE

If you had trouble meeting a challenge, try it again another day with fresh ideas. And if you did meet a challenge, still try it again! There is always more than one way to do something. Give yourself new demands and limits to give the task a new twist.

IMAGINATION

INSPIRATION

COLLABORATION

PROBLEM-SOLVING

BEYOND THE MAKERSPACE

You can use your makerspace toolbox to take on everyday challenges, such as building a battery or wiring a clock. But electrical engineers use the same toolbox to do big things. One day, these tools could help **design** robots that fly planes or circuits to power electronic human organs. Turn your world into a makerspace challenge! What problems could you solve?

GLOSSARY

appliance – a machine that does a special job.

billion – a very large number. One billion is also written 1,000,000,000.

collaboration – the act of working with another person or group in order to do something or reach a goal.

complicated – having many parts, details, ideas, or functions.

design – to plan how something will appear or work.

detail – a small part of something.

develop – to help design or create something.

friction – the resistance between two surfaces that are touching each other.

horizontally – with the long edge in the same direction as the ground.

satellite – a manufactured object that orbits Earth.

solution – an answer to, or a way to solve, a problem.

stadium – a large building with an open area for sporting events surrounded by rows of seats.

technique – a method or style in which something is done.

version – a different form or type from the original.

vertically – with the long edge in the opposite direction from the ground.

vibrate – to make very small, quick movements back and forth. These movements are vibrations.

volt – a unit for measuring the power of an electric current. The number of volts a current uses is its voltage.